Brushing Well

by Helen Frost

Consulting Editor:
Gail Saunders-Smith, Ph.D.

Consultant:
Karen Masbaum Yoder, RDH, Ph.D.
Indiana University
School of Dentistry

Pebble Books

an imprint of Capstone Press
Mankato, Minnesota

Pebble Books are published by Capstone Press
151 Good Counsel Drive, P.O. Box 669, Mankato, Minnesota 56002
www.capstonepress.com

2 3 4 5 6 7 08 07 06 05 04 03

Library of Congress Cataloging-in-Publication Data
Frost, Helen, 1949–
  Brushing well / by Helen Frost.
  p. cm.—(Dental health)
  Summary: A simple description of how to brush your teeth, from putting the
toothpaste on the brush to swishing water in your mouth and spitting at the end.
  ISBN-13: 978-0-7368-0112-6 (hardcover)
  ISBN-10: 0-7368-0112-X (hardcover)
  ISBN-13: 978-0-7368-4859-6 (softcover pbk.)
  ISBN-10: 0-7368-4859-2 (softcover pbk.)
  1. Teeth—Care and hygiene—Juvenile literature. 2. Toothbrushes—Juvenile
literature. [1. Teeth—Care and hygiene.] I. Title. II. Series: Frost, Helen, 1949–
Dental health.
RK63.F75 1999
617.6'01—dc2   198-18379

Note to Parents and Teachers

This series supports the health education standards for how to
maintain personal health. This book describes how people brush their
teeth. The photographs support emergent readers in understanding the
text. Repetition of words and phrases helps emergent readers learn new
words. This book introduces emergent readers to vocabulary used in
this subject area. The vocabulary is defined in the Words to Know
section. Emergent readers may need assistance in reading some words
and in using the Table of Contents, Words to Know, Read More,
Internet Sites, and Index/Word List sections of the book.

Table of Contents

You brush your tongue.

You spit.

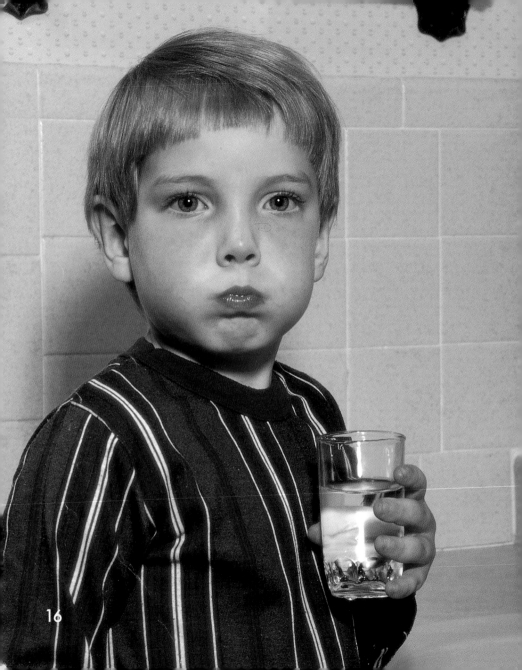

You swish water in
your mouth.

You spit again.

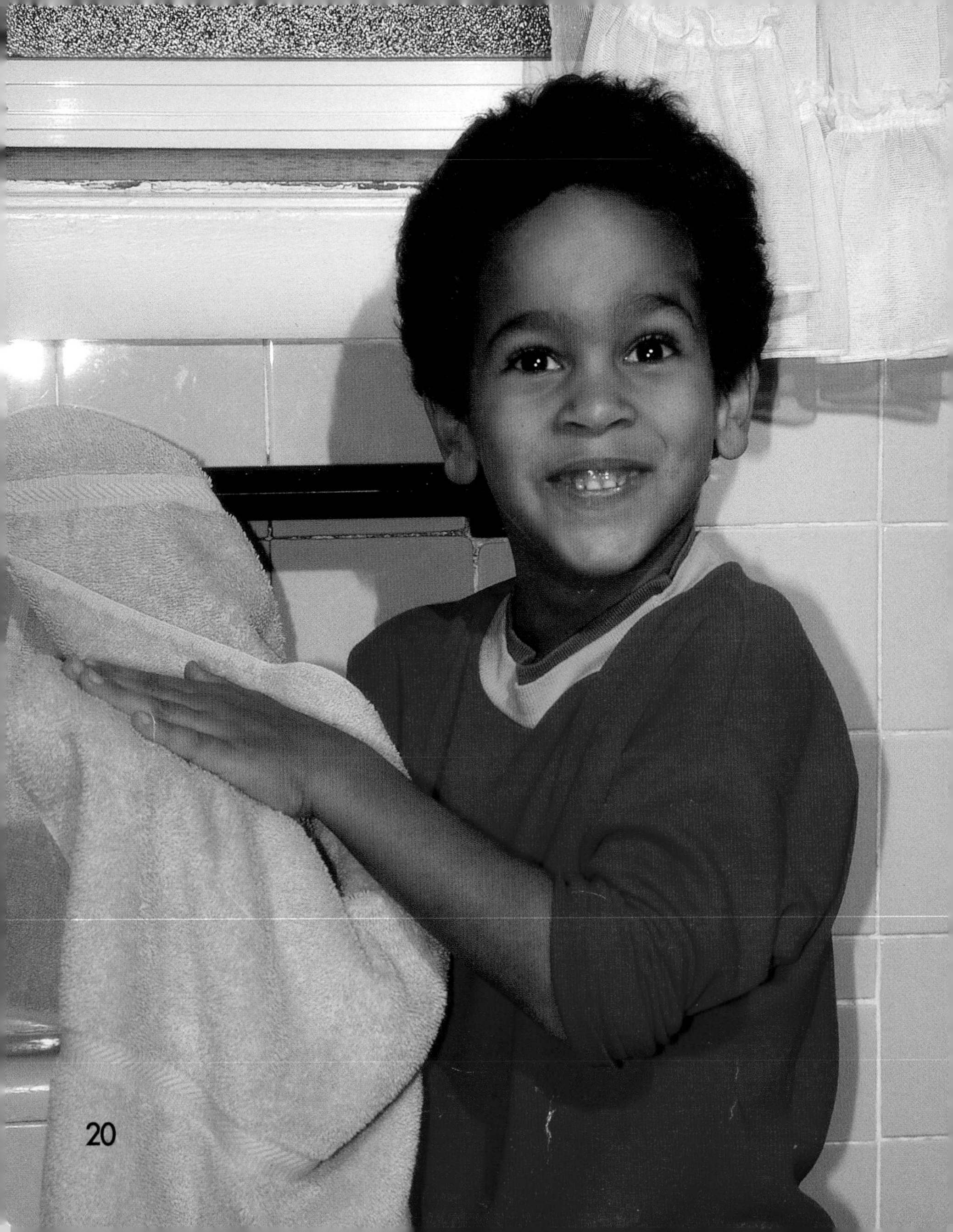

You smile.

Words to Know

brush—to clean your mouth with a toothbrush

spit—to force something out of the mouth; people spit out toothpaste and water when they brush their teeth.

swish—to move with a soft sound; people make a swishing sound with water when they rinse their mouths.

tongue—a movable muscle connected to the bottom of the mouth; dentists say brushing the tongue helps remove food and germs from people's mouths.

toothbrush—a narrow stick with bristles at one end; people use toothbrushes to clean their teeth.

toothpaste—a creamy mixture put on a toothbrush to clean teeth; dentists say people should use a pea-sized drop of toothpaste when they brush.

Read More

Asimov, Isaac, and Carrie Dierks. *Why Do We Need to Brush Our Teeth?* Ask Isaac Asimov. Milwaukee: Gareth Stevens Publishing, 1993.

Gillis, Jennifer Storey. *Tooth Truth: Fun Facts and Projects.* Pownal, Vt.: Storey Communications, 1996.

McGuire, Leslie, and Jean Pidgeon. *Brush Your Teeth Please: A Pop-Up Book.* New York: The Reader's Digest Association, 1993.

Internet Sites

Visit the FactHound at *http://www.facthound.com*

Here's how:

1) Visit the **FactHound** home page.

2) Enter a search word or type in this code: **073680112X**

3) Click on the **Fetch It** button.

Your trusty friend FactHound will fetch the best site for you!

Index/Word List

adult, 5
all, 11
back, 9
brush, 7, 9, 11, 13
front, 7
mouth, 17
puts, 5
sides, 11
smile, 21

spit, 15, 19
swish, 17
teeth, 7, 9, 11
tongue, 13
toothbrush, 5
toothpaste, 5
water, 17
you, 7, 9, 11, 13, 15, 17, 19, 21

Word Count: 42
Early-Intervention Level: 6

Editorial Credits
Colleen Sexton, editor; Clay Schotzko/Icon Productions, cover designer;
    Sheri Gosewisch, photo researcher

Photo Credits
Craig D. Wood, 12, 18
David F. Clobes, 4
David N. Davis, 8
Mark C. Ide, 14
Nancy Ferguson, 16
Photo Network/Earshal Long, cover; Esbin-Anderson, 6, 10
Uniphoto/John Coletti, 1
Valan Photos/V. Wilkinson, 20